ANGRY DAYS

ANGRY DAYS

by Sesshu Foster

West End Press
1987

Grateful acknowledgment is made to the editors of the magazines and books where these poems first appeared: *Alcatraz 3, Amerasia Journal, Ang Katipunan, Black Mountain Review,* BRIGADISTA: HARVEST AND WAR IN NICARAGUA, *Compages, Green Feather, Jacaranda Review, Journal of Ethnic Studies, L.A. Weekly, Long Shot Productions, The Mill Hunk Herald, Minnesota Review, Moosehead Review, Outlaw, Poet's Corner, Quixote, Radical Teacher, Red Bass, The San Fernando Poetry Journal,* SNOW SUMMITS IN THE SUN, *Spectrum, Statement Magazine.*

First edition—September, 1987
ISBN 0-931122-46-5

Artwork by Tom Agawa
Design by Patt Gateley
Typography by Prototype

This project is partially supported by a grant from the California Arts Council, through funding provided by the National Endowment for the Arts, a Federal Agency.

West End Press, Box 291477, Los Angeles, CA 90029

TABLE OF CONTENTS

This book is dedicated to my people,
whose labor, courage and generosity makes my work possible,
to Dolores,
and to our children,
Marina and Umeko,
that they may meet the children of the imprisoned,
the starved, the exploited, the tortured & the disappeared
in a world of their own making.

THE DRY RAIN

LINES IN RED AND WHITE FOR L.A.

1.
Tokyo Rose had already sung her last and
Hearst did not radio the President's answer
from San Simeon. Luther Burbank invented a potato,
Thomas Edison made the thing electric and Alexander
Graham Bell spoke out of it from New York
calling for special wartime collaboration
between Albert Einstein and Charlie Chaplin.
They call this history. Amelia Earhart went down
in a sea of citrus groves drinking a glass of sparkling grapefruit juice
while a cast of thousands sang This Land is Your Land
from Hollywood . . . Most of the United States
was created on a studio backlot behind the railyards,
shipped out at night under the eyes of the Atomic Agency Reagan police,
in nondescript crates stamped BOSTON, RALEIGH, HOUSTON . . .
Special crews of muscular Blacks, Chinese and Indians set up these
huge showpiece burgs and immigrants officiated the efficient return
of the slave labor to prison.
I don't mean that Los Angeles was ever more than a market
for this operation.

2.
Prayers in billfolds and sighs in portfolios,
businessmen wish to have their pituitary gland excised
and replaced by a gold nugget which originally
came from Joaquin Murrieta's head before it melted
inside the Yanqui jar.
His skull the simple Mexican desert,
its silence rings in your ears.
City Hall was the tallest building by the placita
until Sumitomo Bank, ARCO, United California Bank, etc.,
raised their towers above skid row.
Their leaden shadows stick in the faces of the Sunday shoppers
while the sun is left its daily ritual of disembowelment
sliced open by high tension wires,
spilling its guts upon the sizzling streets.

The town looks better, really, at night
the dark hiding the dirty fingers wrapped around
the throat of rivers of the Southwest
the lights fanning out like stars
dumped into the desert from a sky too full
of stars, now too empty.

3.
City,
call it that
as it stands
open to the flies as a corner grocery store.
Put a nickel in the gumball machine chained out front
you can kiss the throat of what's his name?
Murrieta.
As it stands.
City at the end of America, empire
arranged around the Greyhound Station
dreaming the breathless white dream
on the waves at Santa Monica forever west
to Hawaii.   Like Hawaii, California
was only an island, just a shipyard,
without enough elbow room or backbone for concentration camps.
Angel Island lies abandoned,
its institutions rising above the pay parkinglots
of central Los Angeles.

4.
City of the culture of growth and growth of culture of famous
rapist-murderers, and of their newspapers
which glow with the continual reports.
This trash distributed on every streetcorner,
the truckers raise a cloud of concrete particles
which harden into rust-colored air
where further excavations in the vicinity of the sky
may one day reveal along the horizon cream

soft lungs fluttering like white moths.
And the handprints of children appear as petroglyphs
not erasable, everywhere, and all the offices fill with the dust
which falls sideways into their lives
with the staid velocity
of freeway tonnage.

A boy down the street on a bicycle casts the shadow
of the cold eagle of the Sierras.

5.
Ad listed under PERSONALS

To whom it may concern:
Please take the microphone from your squad car
or your personal helicopter and tell
the grandparents of Pennsylvania
we don't want them
littering our freeways with their boys
in trashbags. We have enough to do with Disneyland
so close at hand and so cheap too.

6.
Two girls from Los Angeles:
one nude body was found by the Santa Ana freeway,
the other had been dead for a year at least in
a shallow grave on a hilltop in the neighborhood
where I spent my childhood.

7.
A certain smell:
the black pitch secreted by vibrating telephone poles
during heat waves
the same stuff washes up on beaches at Santa Barbara,
and carries bones
of early horses, giant vultures, sabertooth tigers in pools
by the County Art Museum;

this appears in cracks in the pavement on Santa Monica Boulevard,
Whittier Boulevard all the way
to Gardena, Pasadena, Fullerton, West Covina, and the
San Fernando Valley.
It has the smell of waiting

8.
The smell of waiting in Los Angeles
is most often noticed at bus stops
or riding the bus in crowds battered
by old men who sleep in their clothes.
It drifts from streets where broken down
cars and broken glass glitter in wait
for the children to come home from school and play.
It is in the life of eroded, empty lots.
It could be most characterized by the wrinkled
old man who stood in guaraches, soles
cut of tire treads in the dust, now wearing
tennis shoes made by slave labor in South Korea
and watching the traffic for a chance to cross the street.
Next to him the dog run over and lying corrupt
beside the freeway onramp smells less
of waiting

9.
Happily the rain runs
along your gutters past the County General Hospital of Happiness
where it makes a dry pattering of happiness
and slips into the storm drain
full of these happinesses:
stacks of car bodies to be compacted
an empty bottle upright/ in a soaked paper sack/ on a bench
excrement under a bridge
houses with smashed windows/ floors piled with rotting garbage
bars and strip joints
yards of dusty weeds

perfectly arranged, perfectly attended flower gardens
everything behind its proper, respective wall.
The dry rain washes everything of its happiness
into the river.
The Los Angeles River is designed
with deep, wide concrete banks
for the very purpose of enabling it to hold
all the happiness of your winters.
And the city around it designed like that river
in summer. When the dry rain coats everything
like cheap makeup and cheap perfume.
The air is full of it as a telephone booth
is full of a man who smokes a pack of cigarettes,
a mouthful of chicharrones.
Dear lady for our thirst you give us
lovers' dogs in parks
the serious thoughts of parkingmeters
and the serious intentions of meter maids
and receptionists who take their duties seriously.
Virgin, in your hour of mercy,
which was the lunch hour, you appeared
in the halo of our want to ask for menudo
and when you were told there was none till Sunday
you gave us the public school system
derived from men's faces squashed on the floortiles of restrooms
open to the public in service stations and the county jail,
with the background chorus of beaten women behind
the potted plants and the hurried attendance of automobile accidents,
and the attitude of row after row of broad female backs
leaning over dimly lit needles surrounded by the faces
of children as plentiful as copper pennies,
to you.
I realize I may not appear as respectful as I could be,
but I want to see your hands,
for the night of the river of the city of angels
is getting full of childhoods,

our lady whose embrace is that of nightsticks.

10.
The high schools were all named
after Anglo U.S. presidents so
why not soup or toothpaste brand names?
In its way the city memorializes Brecht every time
it levels another block of poor housing
for an institutional parkinglot.
For instance, in Chavez Ravine they wiped out
a whole ramshackle neighborhood to build Dodger Stadium,
and when the stands are empty and the diamond is silent,
above the sound of the Golden State freeway can be heard
something like distant laughter,
the cough of Carlos Bulosan.
Luckily for him when he died of TB
he was buried in Seattle.
But the faces of people like him are like the land,
they are always in the sun here, even those
manhandled by the California Youth Authority
and would have been conquerors but now only
play the electric guitar of angel dust and sing
about that ungrateful bitch, la chingada.

OFF OF 101

The first time he gets out to the West Coast
this guy has got 4 gallons of pink gas in plastic
containers in the front of this little sports car.
He gives me a lift out of Santa Barbara and
wants to know if I want his black leather jacket
or where could he get $5 for plasma.
The first time this guy hits rush hour traffic
on the Hollywood freeway he's trying to do 70 miles
an hour and we both look backwards as
he tries to change lanes, but then the sports car
slams into the back of a stalled station wagon
dead in the road. I was going to hug
the sky through the windshield as my face
smashed apart the mirror. The tires rubbed the
wheel wells as he pulled over and gave information
to the cops. I picked stuff out of my face.
Not a scratch on the other vehicle.
I had a wok for Mom from San Francisco and
all my other gear in the back seat, and
when he got back, I directed him to County General.
He said it was no problem to wait while
they fixed up my face. The doctor thought
I'd been fighting and had gotten the bad end
of it, but he never did bill me for it.
When I walked down the wide steps of that monument
to the shit hitting the fan, the punk
from Florida and all my stuff were gone.
With the clots stitching my face to the blue
evening, I had to call Jimmy for a ride.
It was late by then, and as we drove down
the San Bernadino through the fog I told him
what happened and he was depressed.
So I told him about sleeping on Garrapatas Beach
and how about an hour before dawn the tide rose
and covered the beach, pouring down my neck
into my sleepingbag like an ice bath,

leaping up to stand in the campfire
spread out on the sand like stars, and
my gear stranded all down the beach in puddles.
And that made Jimmy happy.
And later in the evening we all sat around the livingroom
and I showed you my new nose and you laughed.

NATURAL HISTORY OF THE EASTERN AVENUE EXIT
OFF THE SAN BERNADINO

During the war the Moratorium was in the streets
and we ran through these houses 'children
at play' I tossed a chair through the picture window
and a television set down the stairs,
the homes had been condemned by the prosperity to come:
razed and raised up over the lots three gas stations
and a McDonalds. It was here
two helicopters and five cop cars escorted us
off the property. To be thirteen years old:
watching students blocking traffic on the overpass
retreat before a wall of black leather cops behind plexiglass
shin to chin shields wielding clubs.
Across the street by the bus stop I talked to Victor
for the last time after he was kicked out of high school
for getting shot in a liquor store robbery.
(The life in the street makes the steel belted radials
hum, it makes them hiss in wet weather.)
I'm watching the cop car go through the intersection
and out on the overpass where Ernie and Paul
were picked up for throwing rocks at trucks on the freeway.
The Vietnamese watches me from the register,
standing in the stink of gasoline,
putting $5 into the tank. My registration
expired about a year ago (the cops gone east)
the Toyota's only got one headlight, no spare,
windshield wipers don't work, but I need the car
if I'm going to. On the brick wall between the gas
station and the offramp (where we painted EL SALVADOR
VENCERA at 2 AM) there's the payphone where the kid was
shot, making his last phonecall: sometimes I think
of him when I'm on my doorstep fumbling with my keys
and the phone inside stops ringing.
Ernie the wino died a few yards away, puking
his guts out in the men's restroom. Mornings
on the way to school he'd be lying on the sidewalk,

but he'd get thirsty in the afternoon heat, so
he'd smile toothless behind burnt, scraped skin
and ask for change. The cops swept him up bright and early
—behind the hill they're administering Blacks and Chicanos
in Sybil Brand and Biscailuz, out of sight.
(Like the class which sends our bills and collects on them,
collects our taxes and lives off them:
none of them live in this neighborhood.)
Probably the Vietnamese handing me $5 change
lives in Monterey Park / knows nothing of Willie Herron's
fine mural in the alley behind Plaza Market /
or the hour of contemplation at 1 AM
when the crimson neon bail bonds sign (OPEN 24 HOURS)
blinks on and off.
He came after the war.

HOMES

here he comes. Jimmy
spent a December keeping this guy
from suicide, and here he comes
again. Since he can't recognize
you anymore, he better grin . . .
This guy (skinny from drugs, with
that wasted face, when he was a kid
his folks threw him in jail, and
since then it's been petty theft
and car theft, drugs and time, sleeping
in cars along the street, and
up the sidewalk he slouches
feeling the brick wall like looking
for an out) and somebody named Cardoza
went into the greenhouse (we used to
see from the bus on the way to school,
when we were kids) where this old white
man lived at the bottom of the hill,
a brightly painted toy train
on the roof, for sale. The old man
lived alone and made toys.
When he didn't tell them where the money was
(supposedly he said there wasn't any) they
tied him to a chair and beat on him,
lighting a fire between his legs.
(This guy could've been our brother.
Wouldn't you have talked him out of suicide?)
The next day a neighbor looked in the
open door. The old man lived a few
days in the hospital. When he was gone
kids smashed out the greenhouse glass
and wrecked the toy train. The place
is now bulldozed, the raw earth dark.
And a few days ago between the foundry
and the railroad tracks they found somebody else
knifed for his wallet. Down at the store

(where my sisters cashiered) where
they buy their liquor they brag about it,
saying the cops are more a danger to us
than to them. So watch yourself.
I hold my girl's hand in mine
walking down the hill to the daycare
center. Here he comes

BOOKED

in the county jail the deputy
knocks the mexican drunk off
the steel bench onto the concrete
floor—the mexican wakes up.
the sandy blonde deputy above him
in the fluorescent light (smug:
$18/hour and all the contempt and disdain
of private property for those
who have none) the mexican
slaps at the deputy's leg and
in comes a second deputy, screaming
cursing in english, to pick him up
by his hair (the mexican too drunk
to read the numbers on his wrist
let alone catch this english) he's slapped
punched, dragged back into the booking area,
slammed up against the wall (again)
where a cuban trustee is obtained to translate
the deputy's curses, directives and ranting.
so begins our night inside.
later, the lot of us being processed
further into the depths of the jail beyond
a number of steel doors in holding tanks:
hear a resounding slamming from the booking area.
one deputy says to the other: markham's
at it again! they chuckle, and momentarily
a medic unlocks the steel door with a clatter
and escorts through yet another mexican
with blood seeping through the gauze
bandage on his face.

LAUNDRY

All night long, near the laundry
and the holding tanks, men following orders
barked out to them: standing nude
banging their shoes together,
their clothes discarded in a pile,
handed a blue jumpsuit by a trustee,
marched to their holding cells for processing,
row after row, all night long,
every night.
In the chemical fumes of the laundry
(the drycleaning machines posted with a notice
warning proper ventilation at all times,
the jail has no open windows:
the proper chemicals fuck with your head)
after half the shift the black trustee, Jim,
looks up from folding clothes and says,
nodding at the long lines of new inmates,
"Every man there is a job lost,
a family broken up, lives screwed up.
There's something wrong here."
They keep marching them in off
the streets, and Rick, the good-natured,
sardonic Indian nods at my partner,
the Chicano gang member who chuckles,
"Hey homes, I'm fucked up. I'm really fucked up."
Rick says, "Watch out for that punk,
he likes it here."

THE CORPSE OF A FORGETFUL MAN WILL SUDDENLY SIT UP AND LOOK AROUND

I know there's going to be a screw-up somewhere
when I die
they'll send me straight to hell (I'll find out why later)
I'll find myself there
not knowing why or what's happening (not really awake)
I'll wake up and it'll be
just like Los Angeles.
Or I'll be the way I used to be
the way some people think I still am
I'll be that way forever and that will
confirm their expectations.
I'll be a terrified snot-nosed boy
on some bantustan, full of worms and fear
from eating trash and other people's shit
and no brothers, no one to tell me the truth
I figure with the way things are going
that's just what I can expect
after getting snuffed by dropping from a windowledge
by cops lurking around the house/yard
and me having forgotten my pants
I'll have to stand in line
with the rest of the dumb dead people
(they'll have a line just for the dumb ones
those ones who forgot their ticket, their I.D.,
their *cedula*, their work permit, their internal passbook)
lots of us types will be there,
you know, just like at the bank
sleepy, unshaven, wondering what the hell
just standing there in the wind and no pants
besides being dead too
I'll have to bum a cigarette
to wear on my lip to look tough. I don't smoke.
Looking smart, one cigarette, no pants and no light.
a warm gray wind blowing a lethal smog down on all of us

(but we're dead, right, so who cares?)
and I'll be thinking: are these people radioactive
and some of these women must be awful
pissed off by the time they get here.
Since you ain't there to say anything
(I'll be forgetting your name soon)
I'll catch the wrong dead train
the wrong way from all the people
like you
I'll get stuck in a stuffy 3rd class car
(the kind the windows don't open and the air conditioning
broken) between the dreary petty bourgeois dead
some racists
some suburban teenagers in despair
                              making sexist remarks out of pure anxiety
some hopeless office workers killed
by stray gunfire from the cops across the street
and who are therefore all the more afraid
they've finally lost their job for good
finally their boss can replace them with fresh faces
finally they may yet lose that careful sense of complacency
. . . and the only ones happy about this situation
are two idiots who can remember every game
between Detroit and the Green Bay Packers.
I mean, there I'll be
and without you,
no way out.
I just know I'll make some terrible error in judgment
—even the patience of the dead wears out—
and hell being a capitalist state
whose cops of death won't allow me any visiting hours
I won't get permission to see you,
not even in photographs.
I won't have the right documents,
they will only let me watch TV.
I'll get cut off forever, and realize

too late I've been counting on you all this time
at critical moments like this
my whole life (now it's all over)
and I won't know what to do.
I'll lose track of time, I'll be lost
walking somewhere through a shopping mall
walking in and out of the plastic shops
looking for something I can afford . . .
As usual, I won't have any money, and it'll be a nice day
sunny and all, with the security guards
in plainclothes watching over the faceless mannikins
and the azure smog
gentle on the parked cars
—you know, everything like it is here,
the only thing
you won't be there
that's all.

THE AMERICAN TORSO

THE FINAL YEARS OF LIL MILAGRO RAMIREZ
Dedicated to Seattle CISPES and Grupo Armar

"Lil Milagro Ramirez was a teacher and former member of the Christian Democratic youth movement, an enthusiastic and driving young woman with a pixie's smile. She was also a member of the national leadership of the National Resistance. On November 26, 1976, she was 'disappeared' by the security forces . . .

"Someone . . . who subsequently escaped from the clandestine cells saw Lil Milagro sometime before the coup [of 1979]. Her hair had grown down to her heels, her face was a skull, her health had been broken by starvation, beatings, repeated rape and a brutal abortion. She was unbent in her political convictions."

> *—El Salvador: The Face of Revolution*
> by Robert Armstrong and Janet Shenk

[Milagro was rumored to have been shot along with hundreds of others known to have survived years of torture in the secret jails. Her body was never found.]

1.
Back in the California Sierra Nevada, tired
of driving, reading about El Salvador.
We'll get out and hike a few days . . .
Fidel Castro said camping is good for you,
teaches you to deal with difficult situations.
The blue sky and the sun on the snow,
the peaks still under snow.
The muddy Feather River goes
over spillways and through turbines
of P.G.&E. power dam after dam.
(My car has performed brilliantly, perhaps

it can also find me a job in L.A.)
The long day of the highway
and the bright moon. Marina says,
"Give Leta some crackers."
"Marina," Dolores says, "Leta is not here."
Marina is two years old—when will she see
Violeta again?

2.
This rocky land where Ishi, the last of the Yahi,
emerged starving (because he was alone) to die
of TB a few years later in a museum in San Francisco.
He taught the professors much, but never
his real name. *Ishi* simply meant man in Yahi,
something which could not be magically used
against him or his lost people. In captivity
Lil Milagro surrendered even less information;
it's said she resisted so long that when they
killed her she did not know what year it was.
This country, which manufactures the
mechanisms of their death, knows too little
of their people, their resistance, their
real names. Such final resistance
against enemies who are our own, also,
gives pause, but the real names of the people
remain in life like the land—magic only
in the tender stone of the upraised fist
in a wilderness of ignorance: across the broken country
the path of struggle leads through time, faces,
cities, destinations, and here, in the dusty greenery
of California live oaks scattering dry leaves along Deer Creek,
humbled by mountains, we,
like the surviving indigenous peoples
and Marxist-Leninist guerrillas
of our America,
make a simple camp.

3.

WARRIOR'S GRASS GROWS IN EL SALVADOR
Note: the poet Basho was traveling through feudal Japan and came upon a
field where skulls in the grass marked a battlefield.   He wrote a haiku
something like: "In the summer grass, the warriors dream."

sometime soon it will be spring
the breeze will be warm
the clouds will pass
the grass will rise fresh, green
in all the fields of the world

the grasshopper will buzz and whirl in an arc of air
to disappear in the silver shimmer of the brook trout

soon,
that rushing quiet
breeze overhead carrying the clouds
toward the mountains, will carry laughter
the children will be playing
in all the fields of the world

running ahead of their parents they'll scare
the mating pheasants from the summer grass

this is the promise
of the organic years given up
by the young fighters
there in the dark, stiff grass
in all the fields where they died
breathing that moment with the sunshine
heavy on their shoulders like the pollen
touch of the dusty bees on the blossoms

the breeze will be warm there
around your shoulders like the calm arm of a comrade
the clouds will pass
light and dark through the vast, human day
and then, once again, you can promise

sometime soon,
it will be spring

4.
Under their instruments
she was the combativity and intelligence of a people
and they were only like ants
tearing away her flesh.
The mosquitos which breed in the shallows
where the darker water lists, feed
off Marina's neck and depart
with more humanity, using that blood
to breed. The rapists and assassins
who take our taxes fuck children and kill
those they touch, but the hope and self-determination
of a people cannot be contained in unlit,
filthy infested cells for the condemned.
This is the century of her struggle,
the final years of captivity,
when a world not human enough
took sacrifices in our name,
to learn the name
Milagro.

5.
The world is full of moonlight,
moonlight caught in the oak leaves.
The raccoon and deer tracks on the bank
fill with shadow, the geese tracks go to the water.
A banana slug curls on the wet rocks
where the creek splashes down to the stream.
The willows in midstream bend under the spring rise:
The highest passes will be clear soon.
The crickets in the brush do not sing her name,
the ants silent everywhere, clustering
on the old horse shit. I

have people asleep in the valley,
mouths shut in darkness,
their hands cupping warm empty air.
On the creek the jobless boys sleep,
beer in the stream, their noisy music shut off.
The fisherman's camp is quiet, the fire
dying down, orange.
The family store out on the highway is closed.
Only I am awake with what I know of hate
for this world, but the morning too
cannot sleep and does not wait.
No one here will breathe a word about her
during these nights as long and dark as her hair.

6.
Symbiotic lichen pitting the rocks.
Two snakes mating entwined stiffly
pulsate glistening and shudder apart,
they look our way.
A bat emerges from the trunk of a big oak,
circles and flies off through these alder.
Blooming, the small pretty flowers of the mountain
and the big butterflies . . .
Birds are singing everywhere, and Marina
plays naked by the rushing stream.
She can read this later if she has time:
"Who was Lil Milagro?"
She was someone's daughter
in El Salvador, my girl.

7.
The sound of water fills fir
trees hundreds of feet tall.
On a rock outcropping above Ishi's Deer Creek:
in eons the stream has
cut its little canyon

and winds through mountains
of rough rock—only a stretch of white
water seen at once, before going
through the trees, around a bend.
The deer above us see us first
and move upslope.
Yet the puma you never see is
more watchful.
And that such gold-flecked eyes watched over
the life of the people.

8.
Take the struggle to its final consequences.
Let us be like her, our resistance
alive to the end.
And the moonlit world of high power
lines and huge pipelines, gaping
clear cuts, fuming mills and whining
turbines, scurrying men like
red and black ants, a snake slithering
from a crack in ring of stones
as a bright fire cools to ashes, and injustice
will not simply exist.
These things will not be the way
things are. Our anger shall not be contained
by words: about this atrocity
nothing can be said intelligent,
in itself and alone. Only united
by action have we meaning together,
our work as against so much now,
for so much now.

AMERICA

The forest is
around me.
Full of green light,
magnificent,
alive—
even as
Che.

BARRIO RIGUERO MASS
Iglesia Santa Maria de Los Angeles, Managua

The mural:
the bleeding boat of Christ
flows, part of the
river here,
Christ's bloody hands
above the guitar
above the bombo
pulsing
throughout the church.
And the Chileans sing,
"Brothers and sisters
you have the power
in your hands."
As dark as mud
the man
who passes out
the chairs.
And the children running in
from the street,
here
most of them
wear shoes.
The woman in green
leans through the door,
her white teeth
at the young man's
ear. . . Her smile bright
in Nicaraguan green—
in militia green—
as the Chilean star
in the internationalists' eyes.

DISTANT SEPTEMBER

The dark soil fertile
the volcanic slopes alive
as your firm tenderness,
even as the walking sticks
and jumping spiders

and the disturbed ground
—broken—under the last
standing water of the rainy season
grows shoots of bright grass,
and you go on working
where you are.

Each day the faces in Managua
la Malinche on a crowded bus
her girls pushing a cart
through the muddy street
smelling of rotten garbage,
past the Mercado Oriental
or waiting for the bus in militia green.
I look for your face there
or Marina's face in the child's
face: their eyes simply innocent
and dark
              Do your days, too,
pass like other days?
Like the clouds over
the Oaxaca valley, you
remember, amid a humble working people?
I string the mosquito net
between two local rocking
chairs and sleep on the floor:
dry lightning over Lake Managua,
thunderstorms at night.
Some fleas and mosquitos
I never see . . . (In the morning
at the training compound under the

large trees behind us, they begin
the day with Nueva Trova
as the big trucks across the carreterra norte
Pedro Joaquin Chamorro—
the northern highway—head out
of the zona franca prison
full of men
for the fields.
Before the triumph, they say
it had been a somocista factory.)
Later, in the fields myself,
Danilo handed me the shovel
saying, "Made in Nicaragua.
It's shit." With the frustration
a legacy of so-called underdevelopment,
I did not suffer as I bent
my back under that
beautiful sky.
The shovel didn't last long,
widening a couple of blisters across
my palm, while the brigadistas
put the eucalyptus and oak trees
in along the row; the sun emerged
out onto our skin
light through the big cumulus
light through the green leaves
of the new plants,
the heat like a hand on our backs
as the creaking shovel turned out
moist sandstone and dark volcanic earth.

After work, riding through the busy capital
in the back of a Toyota truck,
watching for you.

LETTER BEFORE LEAVING FOR
A REFORESTATION BRIGADE

You may not understand
why these duties,
why such travels,
why they are fighting . . .
(I am not going to
fight, my little one,
I told you what kind of
work it is.
You said, "Are they
going to teach you how?"
"How to plant trees?"
"Yes," you said.
"Yes.")
To plant trees
and,
to plant trees.
Right now you nap
at Abuelito's, the smog
blowing through the bougainvillea
at our door . . .
In Nicaragua, I promise
in the rain or in the
heat, with my back
bent over the earth
and my hands in it,
I will be talking
to you,
while little halfmoons of dirt
wax underneath my fingernails.
Our nights you may feel grow far
apart . . . Listen
to me, my girl, and
listen to your mother.
She will have stories
for you, and between us

in pauses in the work
a long time from now
we will have our
little poems.
In time you should
understand, better
than I, I hope, the
love such duties are
responsible for,
for you,
for you and yours.
I'll leave this
in an envelope *(the
mail's no good where I'm
going)* for your mother
to read to you
when I'm gone.
One day you may see
the breadth of the great land
where in a warm winter storm
washing out roads, heaving
huge hemlocks into the flood,
there was this beautiful strong
young woman hiking for miles
with Jimmy and me
through the rising rivers
to the shore, where we watched
trees float past the fishing village
out to sea, the rain
beating on us in sheets
and the logs booming together
in the surf as it grew dark.
The time was upon us, you
were coming and we didn't know.
Her full cheeks flushed
under those dark eyes, that

young wife's arms around my neck
as we went through
the cold brown flood.
You were born that night
after a rough ride driving
the little Fiat through streams
toward the highway along the
Hoh (said to be Quileute
meaning Great Milky River)
with Jimmy holding her hand.
In the lumbertown clinic
she was so happy she didn't
sleep all night, still
holding you in the morning
when Jimmy and I awoke in the car,
big black ravens scraping the remains
of butter forgotten on the hood.
That day, like a kid's storybook,
the sky cleared and the sun came out
on the steaming rainforest.
You slept in your mother's arms.
I will not be there when you have
to ask this of yourself: what
responsibility have I alone,
amid the duties called for
in the rough, great land?
Marina, you were such a child
born in a warm storm,
with the necessary blood,
the necessary cries.
Even now I miss you.
Even now the Hoh River
carries glacial silt
milked from the high
mountainsides to the sea.

THE WORLD WE GIVE OUR CHILDREN

REALPOLITICS:
THE WORLD WE GIVE OUR CHILDREN

Heading west on the Santa Monica, Peter Gabriel's
"Biko" on the cassette, so Marina asks, (age 5)
"Why did they make a song about Biko?"
"Because he died, Hoh."
"Did the white people kill him?"
Eyes on traffic, "Yes, Hoh."
"Is it white people singing the song?"
"Yes."
"Why do the white people sing about him if they killed him?"
"Not all white people are bad.
Your grandpa is a white man, isn't he?"
"Yeah."
And after a moment, "Grandpa's not so bad.
He's not a killer. Because he's not young,
like us."
"Yeah, Hoh?"
"Yeah."

DREAM

we were going through a high mountain valley in the late afternoon
it was early winter, there wasn't much snow yet
but there would be soon, as the central drainage
was covered, the water flowing underneath
we went on horseback through bare alder
aspen and willows naked against the overcast sky
we discussed the trail with destination in mind
wagon ruts could be seen criss-crossing
in the bent yellow and green grass yet lush
(it must have been a good summer) between patches of snow
the snow creaking as we pushed through
the sound of our voices at once muffled by the cloudy cold
and yet magnified by the quality of silence
the mountains hold as they grow dark in twilight
everyone's breath coming out in plumes
heavy with the promise of weather
above the thudding effort of the horses
hearing voices we spurred on
believing more of our people ahead
the brush snapped at our passage as we emerged
into a clearing where we faltered, horses clumsy with fear
we rode under a great black structure like a railroad trestle
constructed of timbers steeped in tar and joined together by great
ropes like a gigantic corral about us and on its heights
against the stars men were hanging, tied to the timbers
as if crucified, people shrouded from head to foot in black
and tied with thick ropes to the timbers which were ablaze
set afire at separate points even as panic-stricken hoofbeats
fled with the shouts of men and other men in shrouds
standing above us with torches

YOUR PRESENCE IN CUBA

An absent face, a voice away.

Marina played with the very small
crabs, blue and green
waiting for the ride
to save their rocks from her hands and mine.
Hazy days, living by collecting unemployment, which
among other more dubious advantages
allows you time to do the dishes.
(*Capital*, volume one, open at page
292.)
Living out of boxes,
in and out of the beat-up car,
in and out of the apartment door.
I wish all the clothes hanging
in the closet or folded on the shelf were
full of people, especially children.
Age 2, Marina is too alone
for us to run off to the mountains.
        She said her Mami is at "werk,"
and when showed the juvenile book
(published in the U.S.) about Cuba
she said one dancer was her Mami,
and another was Moyra,
before she napped.
        She does not ask where Dolores is.
Silvio Rodriguez singing, solo
precision guitar playing.
And the sky overcast after a brilliant week.
And the mountains in back of us,
folding away like centuries of trees and rocks,
foggy with ravens, splintered with hawks,
to the rolling plains.
The whole country at our backs:
the pressure of its prejudices,
the petty ugliness until death,

its shifty chances all up and down the street,
like the gravity of stones
blistering my feet.
Marina on my shoulders.
        "Hello Mami, hello Mami," she called
into the speakers with the stereo
cassette recording of Dolores on, she
pressed up against the black, trying to get in:
"Hello Mami?
Goodbye."
(Leaving Seattle, but remaining while waiting.)
The mountains above us
heavy snow, blasted
frozen rock.
The country about us private
(the property of the past),
engorged with lifetimes.
Great-grandmother Alberta Buell is
83, I don't remember our grandfather's
first name but after she married him
Grandma played piano during silent
movies at a downtown theater in L.A.,
and she still plays the organ.
She lives alone and is lonely.
This is the North American geography
of our quietude in the face of
a daily alienation.
Below California, that island,
the Indians are being slaughtered,
men, women and children whose crystalline
voices never pierce our
bed of sedimentary isolation.
Our mortality grows mute,
our normality falls in shadow,
a lapidary process.
Birds as beautiful as the quetzal fly

deeper into the retreating rainforest.
We still have time.
A New York Jew who was a neighbor
when she called me a "brave person"
meant only to compliment the way I stood
in the tall solitude of the days
that follow the singular night
of this society.
Perhaps she was talking about the way
the city makes me thin.
          (I could not jump the barbwire
fence at the zoo with Marina, riding
my shoulders, besides, the cops
cruise the parkinglot to crucify you
for just such a sin.)
Friends are sympathetic,
the family would help.
But, on the other side of the coin,
they are all economically integrated,
having (or not having, as the case may be)
their own bank accounts, driver's
licenses, social security numbers,
their own lives leading along
the road to final exploitation.
And, at this point, the door open
reminds me of the distance
not that we traveled, for we
have not come far enough, but
that space which has come
to be a part of us.
          Marina is now awake, and, you
know, no letters are allowed through to Cuba.

JULY

I see in the shimmering
baby heat your
down-turned mouth

the purple of a thistle
spiny on the roadside
webs turgid with dust

what you want
rises in the baby sun
stiff as the corona of eucalyptus

on the baby hill, coming
up together in the broad
daylight transfixed by your walking

I cannot grasp
this motion so sure and random
as babies, butterflies

whose foreshortened heavy
hour uplifts passion
like the uncashable

unemployment check.

GRANDPA

ACROSS THE STREET FROM THE CEMETERY WHERE GRANDPA
PLANTED BODIES AND GRASS ONE DARK THANKSGIVING
NIGHT THE BARTENDER OFFERED THE REGULARS THE
CHOICE OF AN OUZO OR A BUSHMILL'S. GRANDPA TOOK
THE BUSHMILL'S. THEN HE TOLD ME THIS STORY OF THE
WORKERS. THEY WERE A BUNCH OF BAD-MOUTHED
MISFITS, BIGOTS AND LOSERS DOING ALL THE GRAVEYARD
LABOR FOR $4/HOUR. ONE RAINY DAY THEY WERE ASSIGNED
TO PLANT A PAUPER FOR THE COUNTY, AN INDIGENT OLD
LADY WHO PAID NO MONEY TO DIE, RUNNING OUT OF BOTH
CASH AND BREATH WITHOUT PERMISSION. THE PAUPERS
WERE BURIED ON THE UNMARKED HILLSIDE BEHIND THE
CEMETERY PROPER, SO THE CREW LOADED THE PINE BOX
ONTO THE TRUCK AND DROVE UP TO WHERE THE LANE
ENDED IN THE MUD. IN THE POURING RAIN THOSE MIDDLE-
AGED MEN, BEATEN RACISTS, MALCONTENTS, BOOZERS ALL,
WITH THEIR WHINING PUT-DOWNS OF EVERYTHING AND
EVERYBODY, WHICH GRANDPA SAID HE HATED WORST OF
ALL, LIFTED THE COFFIN BETWEEN THEM, TWO ON EACH
END AND STARTED UPHILL. THEY WERE IN MUD TO THEIR
ANKLES AND THE RAIN WAS BEATING ON THEM, SOAKING
THEM TO THE SKIN IN MINUTES. ONE OF THE GUYS, CALL
HIM EDDIE, WAS THE BUTT OF HALF THEIR JOKES BECAUSE
HE WAS NOT ALL THERE, HE WAS RETARDED, AND HE
SHOWED THEM UP BY DOING JUST AS GOOD A JOB AS ALL
THE REST. MAYBE IT WAS EDDIE, BUT SOMEBODY SLIPPED
AND THE COFFIN WENT DOWN IN THAT MESS OF SPLATTER-
ING CLAY. IT WAS HEAVY AND THEY HAD TO LET IT GO OR
GO WITH IT THEMSELVES. THE PINE BOX WENT DOWN ON
ITS SIDE AND THE LID CAME OFF; THE OLD WOMAN'S BLACK
LEG FELL OUT, PERFECTLY NAKED IN THE RAIN. EDDIE
LOOKED DOWN AT IT AND SAID, "I DON'T RECOGNIZE HER."
AND THEY LOOKED AT THE LEG AND LOOKED AT EDDIE
AND STOOD AROUND LAUGHING IN THE RAIN. AND I
LAUGHED TOO OVER MY GIN AND TONIC.

WHY IS GRANDPA'S FACE SO RED, MARINA? DID HE FORGET
HIS HAT WHILE PLANTING ORANGE TREES IN DEATH VALLEY
AND GET SUNBURNT ALL THE WAY BACK? WHY CAN'T HE
SIT STILL, MARINA, DOES HE CARRY A LIVE WIRE IN HIS
POCKET FULL OF HOLES? ARE HIS SHOES SO THIN FROM
HITTING THE STREET THAT HE CAN'T BEAR TO WAIT ON
ETERNITY FOR EVEN A FEW MINUTES? THE WAY THE
DISTANCE RINGS IN OFF THE LAND MAKES HIM SQUINT,
AND WHEN HE GRITS THE TEETH HE HAS LEFT YOU CAN
TELL HE DOESN'T LIKE IT AT ALL. TELL UMEKO HIS NAME IS
FOSTER, TOO, BECAUSE HE'S HER GRANDPA, TOO. IN SPITE
OF THE MISSING TEETH THE GRIN IS STILL WHAT WAS
CALLED RADIANT, AND HE DOES HAVE NEW ARTIFICIAL
TEETH. YOU WERE THREE WHEN YOU FIRST MET HIM IN SAN
JOSE, WHERE HE SLEPT IN A CAR IN A GARAGE AND GOT
DRUNK WITH THE INDIANS AND DOLORES GAVE HIM A
HAIRCUT IN THE GARDEN WHERE HE WAS WORKING. IF
YOU'RE LUCKY YOU'LL HAVE GRANDPA'S HANDS: HANDS
THAT ALMOST HELPLESSLY MAKE THINGS GROW, HANDS
HAPPIER AND STRONGER THAN THE MAN. GRANDPA CAN
TELL YOU THESE STORIES BETTER THAN I—THE TROUBLE
WITH HIS STORIES IS THAT THEY ARE TRUE. I'LL WRITE THIS
HERE NOW IN THE HOT RAIN IN L.A. IN JULY 1986 BECAUSE
SOMETHING MAY HAPPEN TO GRANDPA BEFORE YOU ARE
OLD ENOUGH TO UNDERSTAND, BECAUSE SOMETHING IS
ALWAYS HAPPENING TO GRANDPA.

GRANDPA GREW UP ON THE BARBARY COAST BUT IT WAS
GONE WHEN HE GOT BACK FROM THE WAR, WHERE THE
FRESH SEA BREEZE BLOWS ACROSS THAT HILLY TOWN
WHERE HIS FATHER LIKE SO MANY OTHERS WORKED AWAY
HIS DAYS IN THE SHIPYARD, AND GRANDPA USED THE WAR
TO RUN OFF TO STRING TELEPHONE WIRES ACROSS NORTH
AFRICA AND RETURNED TO AMERICA ON TOP OF THE
WORLD WITH AN ITALIAN GIRL WHO WANTED TO MARRY A
RICH AMERICAN AND BOY WHEN SHE PICKED GRANDPA DID

SHE MAKE A MISTAKE. HE WANTED TO BE A PAINTER, TO MAKE IT THE SUPREME SINGLE ACT THAT SET HIM FREE. HE STUDIED PAINTING IN ITALY AT THE ACADEMIA DE BELLE ARTE DI NAPOLI WHERE NO MATTER HOW MANY TIMES THEY CHANGED MODELS HE PAINTED THE SAME PAINTING ON THE SAME CANVAS SO THEY MADE HIM PAINT OUT IN THE HALL. HE PAINTED LOTS OF PAINTINGS BUT NEVER KEPT ANY OF THEM: LIKE YOUR OTHER GRANDPA DID IN MEXICO WITH A CAMERA NOW BIG AND BLACK AND DUSTY LIKE A STRANGE ACCORDION OR ONE-EYED ALLIGATOR IN THE CLOSET NEVER TO MAKE MUSIC AGAIN. SO YOU KNOW NOW WHO TO BLAME WHEN YOU GET THOSE FEELINGS, TERRIBLE FUNNY FEELINGS OF WANTING TO BE "FURTHER BOUNDLESS EVERYWHICHWAY" FREE WHILE EVERYBODY ELSE THINKS YOU ARE IMPRACTICAL IF NOT COMPLETELY IRRESPONSIBLE WHEN THE CHARM WEARS OFF.

GRANDPA DID EVERYTHING FROM PICKING FRUIT, SECURITY GUARD, DRIVING AN AMBULANCE, MAKING FISH STICKS, FIXING RAILROAD BRIDGES, GARDENING, FOREMAN OF LANDSCAPING CREWS, GROUNDSKEEPER, AND MAY REMEMBER HIS DAYS TOO WELL IN THE MERCHANT MARINE AS DISHWASHER GOING AROUND THE WORLD ONCE OR TWICE AND THAT'S WHY HE WALKS LIKE A BOXER AND HAS A FACE LIKE THE ROCKY MOUNTAINS. HE SPENT DAYS AND WEEKS IN UNEMPLOYMENT OFFICES AND ON THE STREETS RUNNING DOWN WANT ADS AND HE'D END UP HANDING OUT ADVERTISEMENT FLYERS FOR ENOUGH TO PAY RENT AND BEER YET NEVER WOULD KNOW WHAT THE WORD "PROLETARIAN" MEANT. WIFE #1 TOOK BABY ALBERTA BACK TO ITALY AND LATER DID MARRY AN AMERICAN MILLIONAIRE AND TRIED TO GET GRANDPA TO TAKE BACK HIS NAME FOR $3,000 BUT WHEN THE MESSENGER CAME TO THE DOOR GRANDPA TOLD HIM NO, SO NOW YOU KNOW ABOUT HOW MUCH YOUR NAME IS WORTH TO THE RICH NOT TO HAVE AND THAT HAS TO BE WORTH SOMETHING. GRANDPA

MARRIED GRANDMA IN A ZEN CHAPEL IN SANTA BARBARA
FULL OF IRISES AND LILIES CUT FROM THE ESTATE HE
GARDENED AND THE WHOLE CARAVAN OF FRIENDS HEADED
UP INTO THE HILLS AFTERWARDS FOR A BARBECUE. HE
WAS ALWAYS GOOD AT THINGS THAT WERE REAL NICE FOR
ONE DAY.

WHEN THE KIDS CAME GRANDPA DID ALL KINDS OF LITTLE
JOBS IN LITTLE TOWNS ALL OVER CALIFORNIA (SIGNING A
DIFFRENT OCCUPATION ON ALL OUR BIRTH CERTIFICATES)
AND WE LIVED IN MOUNTAINS AND FOOTHILLS, IN THE
ORCHARDS AND TOWNS; WE NEVER HAD TOO MUCH TO EAT
IN THOSE LITTLE TOWNS WHERE GRANDMA WENT LOOK-
ING FOR HIM IN THE BARS ON PAYDAY AND HE WAS ALWAYS
THINKING UP OTHER GOOD REASONS FOR HEADING DOWN
THAT LONG HIGHWAY WHERE THE SOUND OF THE HORNS
OF SEMIS AT NIGHT ON THE EDGE OF TOWN BECAME THE
SONG OF MY CHILDHOOD. YOUR GREAT-GRANDMOTHER
UMEKO AGAWA TOLD GRANDMA, "HE'S AN ALCOHOLIC—
YOU'RE GOING TO HAVE TROUBLE WITH HIM" AND SHE WAS
RIGHT, BUT GRANDMA MARRIED HIM ANYWAY. HE WAS
ALWAYS PRONE TO SUPERLATIVES IN HIS SPEECH ON
EVERYTHING FROM HER LEG OF LAMB TO QUOTIDIAN
WONDERS AND CHAINS TO TOMORROW'S PLANS AND THE
DOCTORS TOLD HIM HIS DRINKING WAS GOING TO KILL HIM
IN TEN YEARS BUT HE'D NEVER STOP IN THIS WORLD AND
HE'S STILL HERE (AND YOU CAN SEE FOR YOURSELF WHAT
KIND OF WORLD IT IS). THE LAST TIME I LIVED WITH HIM
WAS WHEN I WAS EIGHT AND GRANDMA WIPED THE BLOOD
OFF HER FACE AND PUT THE SIX OF US IN THE CAR (SHE WAS
PREGNANT WITH YOUR UNCLE SABBY) AND WE LOOKED
OUT OF THE BACK WINDOW AS SHE DROVE OFF AND THE
COPS WERE PUTTING THE HANDCUFFS ON HIM AND HE
LOOKED UP, SAW US LOOKING AT HIM, SO HE GRINNED.

GRANDPA STILL DRINKS SOME UGLY SHIT LIKE GREEN
HUNGARIAN WINE AND CHEAP SOUR CALIFORNIA RED
WINE AND BEER AFTER BEER AFTER BEER (FIRST THING IN
THE MORNING) AND THAT'S WHY WHEN ALL OF HIS WIVES
ONE AFTER THE OTHER SAID GIVE UP THE BOTTLE OR ME,
THAT WAS THAT, THEY NEVER HAD A CHANCE. AFTER THE
DIVORCE GRANDMA RAISED YOUR SEVEN AUNTS AND
UNCLES ALONE WORKING IN THE DAY AND GOING TO
SCHOOL AT NIGHT AND GRANDPA WOULD ONLY SEND A
FEW HUNDRED DOLLARS NOW AND THEN. HE'D SHOW UP
DRUNK WHEN I WAS WITH MY FRIENDS AND THEY'D GET
QUIET AND HE'D BE GRINNING AND I'D GET MAD BUT THEY
KNEW BETTER THAN TO SAY ANYTHING. KNOW THIS,
MARINA: WHEN SOMEONE SMUG THAT YOU'RE WITH
MAKES FUN OF THE POOR BASTARDS DIGGING DITCHES IN
THE NOONDAY SUN OR WEAVING THROUGH THE CROWD
AIMLESS OR BRUSHING OFF SOME OLD MAN THEY ARE
MAKING FUN OF MEN LIKE YOUR GRANDFATHER. WHEN I
WAS IN JUNIOR HIGH SCHOOL HE BOUGHT ME A TYPE-
WRITER FROM PERU, SENT ME JAPANESE MONEY, AND
WROTE ME A LETTER FROM VIETNAM: LIFE WAS ALWAYS LIKE
A MERRY-GO-ROUND BROKEN LOOSE, HE WAS ALWAYS
TRYING TO RID HIS HIGH HORSE FREE AND IN THIS YOUR
AUNT NAOMI AND YOUR UNCLE PAUL AND ME HAVE
SOMETHING IN COMMON, THOUGH WE CAN DENY IT AS
GRANDPA CAN TOO, BUT IF HE THINKS ME UNNECESSARY
AND MEAN FOR WRITING YOU THIS HE MIGHT DO WELL TO
ASK HIMSELF WHY. I'LL BE FOREVER LOOKING THROUGH
THOSE DIMLY LIT BARS FOR THAT OLD MAN, WHERE THE
SUNLIGHT FALLS YELLOW THROUGH A CRACK IN THE
PLATEGLASS AND IT TAKES A MOMENT FOR YOUR EYES TO
ADJUST TO THE RAY OF SWIRLING DUST BEHIND THE BEER
SIGN AND THE OTHER SMASHED MEN PAUSE BEFORE HE
LAUGHS AND CLAPS ME ON THE SHOULDER AND MAKES A
ROUND OF INTRODUCTIONS.

GRANDPA GOT SHOT IN WATTS ABOUT THE TIME OF THE
RIOTS BY A BLACK KID WITH A HIGH-POWERED RIFLE AS HE
DROVE A TRACTOR IN AN L.A. CITY SCHOOLS SCIENCE
CENTER, AND THE KID SHOT AT EVERYBODY ELSE ON THE
STREET, TOO. THE BULLET BROKE BOTH HIS LEGS AND HE
SPENT NINE MONTHS IN A CAST FROM CHEST TO TOES,
WITH HIS GIRLFRIEND BUNNY SMUGGLING HIM BOTTLES
AND DELIVERING US FOR VISITS. THERE HE TOLD US HOW
THE TRACTOR WENT OFF BY ITSELF ACROSS THE FIELD AND
HE COULD HEAR HIS CO-WORKERS CHASING IT DOWN AS
HE LAY THERE ON THE GROUND. AFTER THEY TOOK THE
PINS OUT OF HIS LEGS AND TAUGHT HIM HOW TO WALK
AGAIN HE WENT TO NICARAGUA WITH AN OUTFIT CALLING
ITSELF EXPEDITIONS UNLIMITED INC. TO STUDY INDIAN
RUINS IN THE JUNGLE (HE THOUGHT) AND SAMPLE
BROMELIADS BUT THE STORY GOES THAT THEY TOOK
EVERYONE'S MONEY AND LEFT THEM STRANDED, SO AFTER
HE SAW THE REST BACK TO THE STATES GRANDPA SPENT A
YEAR THERE IN THE STREETS OF SOMOZA'S MANAGUA
(BEFORE THE EARTHQUAKE, BEFORE THE TRIUMPH) AND HE
BROUGHT BACK WIFE #3 OWING EVERYBODY MORE MONEY
THAN EVER. AUNT CARMEN WAS BORN IN CALIFORNIA
AND FOR AWHILE THEY WERE A HAPPY FAMILY WITH HIS
NEW JOB, A NEW SUIT AND A NEW CAR, BUT IT COULDN'T
LAST: TINA GAVE HIM THE ULTIMATUM AND HE THREW IT
ALL AWAY. WHEN I ASKED HIM WHAT HAPPENED TO THE
CAR HE SAID HE DROVE IT INTO A FIELD ONE NIGHT AND
WALKED AWAY AND NEVER WENT BACK FOR IT, AND THE
SUIT ENDED UP IN BOXES SOMEWHERE WHICH NEVER GOT
FORWARDED WHEN HE MOVED ON. IT WAS 1977 AND THE
INSURRECTIONAL WAR IN NICARAGUA BY THE SANDINISTAS
AGAINST THE SOMOZA DICTATORSHIP WAS HEATING UP, SO
THE INS FOUND OUT THEY WERE NO LONGER TOGETHER
AND TRIED TO DEPORT TINA AND CARMEN BACK TO
NICARAGUA (THOUGH OF COURSE CARMEN HAD NEVER
BEEN THERE) AND I RODE THE GREYHOUND BACK AND
FORTH THROUGH OAKLAND, VALLEJO, FAIRFIELD AND
VACAVILLE CARRYING MESSAGES BETWEEN GRANDPA AND

HIS FAMILY, TRYING TO GET HIM TO HELP TINA GET THE
GOVERNMENT OFF HER BACK BUT THE PERSON WHO DID
THE MOST WAS EIGHT-YEAR-OLD CARMEN WHO TRANS-
LATED FOR HER MOTHER AND TOOK CARE OF THEM AND
HER NEW-BORN SISTER VERONICA. AND WHERE IS CARMEN
NOW, GRANDPA? HE WORKED AS A SHIT-GRINDER IN A
FERTILIZER FACTORY, DUG HOLES IN THE GRAVEYARD,
LANDSCAPED TRACT HOMES, READ ZEN MANUALS AND
POETRY, NOVELS AND OTHER BOOKS AND NEVER GOT ANY
POLITICS, REMAINED ALWAYS CONFUSED, ALWAYS ENTHUSI-
ASTIC, DRANK WITH HIS MEXICAN CREWS AT HOME AND IN
THE BARS, EYED THEIR DARK PRETTY DAUGHTERS, BUT
GRANDPA WAS NO LONGER THAT COLLEGIATE BOXER IN
CHICO ON THE G.I. BILL, NO LONGER THE CHARISMATIC
BOHEMIAN ARTIST TYPE, HIS HAIR TURNED COMPLETELY
WHITE AND MORE TEETH FELL OUT SO THAT NO TWO
TOUCHED EACH OTHER ANY LONGER, A GANG OF BLACK
KIDS IN THE DYING ALLEYS OF DOWNTOWN VALLEJO TRIED
TO BEAT HIM TO DEATH BUT HE KEPT HIS HEAD DOWN AND
STAGGERED AWAY WITH ONLY HIS NOSE BROKEN FOR THE
THIRD OR FOURTH TIME, WHEN I VISITED HIM IN THE
RENTED ROOM ABOVE THE CHINESE RESTAURANT I SAW HE
COULD NO LONGER LIVE THROUGH MORE BEATINGS, HE
WAS PAST SIXTY WHEN HE STAYED WITH PAUL IN SAN JOSE
AND WHEN PAUL LEFT HE WAS BACK IN THE STREETS AGAIN:
HE COULD NO LONGER MAKE ENDS MEET ON DAY-LABOR,
GARDENING AND BREAKING CONCRETE FOR $4/HOUR,
SOMETIMES HIS KNEES AND ANKLES WOULD SWELL UP
FROM GOUT AND HE COULD NO LONGER WALK, WITHOUT
TEETH HE COULD NO LONGER EAT ITALIAN DELICACIES AND
MEAT AND OTHER THINGS, AND AS THE LIFE OF THE STREET
WAS WHAT WAS KILLING HIM THE VETERANS HOSPITAL IN
PALO ALTO SENT GRANDPA TO THE OLD SOLDIERS' HOME IN
YOUNTVILLE IN THE HEART OF THE WINE COUNTRY WHERE
HE MIGHT FINALLY (AS FINAL AS ANYTHING WAS FOR HIM)
MAKE HIMSELF AT HOME (AS MUCH AS HE WAS EVER AT
HOME ANYWHERE, OF HIS OWN MAKING) AND HE COULD
REMAIN AND DRINK, READYING HIMSELF FOR WHATEVER

LUCKLESS SOJOURN HE MIGHT MAKE ANEW ALONG THE
FOREVER-INCREASING FRONTIERS OF HIS OWN HUMAN
LIMITATIONS AS HE WAS ALWAYS UNWILLING TO ACKNOWL-
EDGE EVEN IN HIS MANY LETTERS TO ME (I'VE BOXED THEM
IF YOU WANT TO READ THEM) SHOWING HIS ATTENTION TO
SUNLIGHT AND THE WEATHER, PEOPLE AND ACQUAIN-
TANCES, PLANTS AND COINCIDENCES AND ART, IDEALIST
SPIRITUAL ASPIRATIONS, AS WELL AS A CERTAIN HARD-WON
POETIC BASED ON LIVED EXPERIENCE WE SHARED IN TOWNS
LIKE SANTA ROSA AND SEBASTOPOL, OAKHURST AND LOS
BANOS, HIS ROAD THROUGH LIFE HE RECOUNTS IN HIS
VERNACULAR FROM THE FORTIES AND FIFTIES AS WHEN
DURING THE SIXTIES WE MOVED THROUGH ANOTHER
TOWN, ACROSS A BRIDGE ABOVE A RIVER RUSHING DOWN
THROUGH ROCKS INTO THE OPEN SEA SMELLING OF THE
WET WINTER THROUGH THE OPEN CAR WINDOWS (I
REMEMBER HIS LOUD LAUGH) AND THE ROAD DISAPPEARS
WET AND DARK INTO THE MOUNTAINS, IT'S A WINDING
ROAD, MARINA, THAT YOU AND UMEKO WILL TRAVEL TOO

CALIFORNIA ROLL
For Umeko Agawa

The morning and evening fog
tastes of the ocean
and lies
on the shoulders of the hills.
Already my brothers and I
will have eaten at the common table
enriched by proletarian women
publicly shy.
Their humble shoulders
firm as the hills
under a loaded sky, heavy
with dark clouds of commerce
owned by white strangers, men
who run the business of taking
things out of their hands.
The way asparagus is clipped.
The way leaves are scattered
off the oaks by summer's
desert winds.
Arms tenaciously clasped about
the things they love
like oak roots in the green
hills of winter, when
the growing time is in, their sharp
white smile fresh yet.
Their dark hair tied behind
strong necks, arranging
everything from the road
to the knife, the house and market,
with steady, chapped fingers.
Growing food to feed the children,
how much time was left them?
Bringing it in
in a stride as crisp as carrots,
as spinach stems in a drizzle,

and avocado smooth (as if polished
by the branches
of snow-fed streams down
from the mountain) and smooth, too,
as tears (their responsibility
for the children alone, the unemployed
or drunk man gone, useless
anyway) also smooth of whines,
whimpers, and almost out of breath
with running after the wind.
And heaving a birth into the dark.
And waiting by California
when it was broke, and the men
broke, too, thought up lies
for women warmer than a thousand California
hills in the sunshine.
Taste that sushi now:
the jacket of sun-dried nori
wrapped around the roll
of rice from the Sacramento Valley
(where the heron still stalks his silver reflection
in reeds under an orange sunset)
and the fresh seeds of the cucumber
stick to your teeth, and the avocado
whose stone fits into your palm
and the crab and kamaboko is pressed together
with the sea salt or salt sweat
of those women's hands. That salt
tastes of your own blood
but without the tears
they've suffered.

CHICO?

Chicolife?
Is it getting really Chicolico?
Or Chicoitis?
Or Chicobaboso?
Or Chicoflocoso?
Or Chicomocoso?
Or Chicochistoso?
Or Chicochiquitito
Or Chico-seven-leagues-under-the-sea?
Chico-sinking-into-the-ocean-forever?
Or Chico of the outback?
Or Chico at the base of the Sierras waiting for winter?
Or Chico with babes on bicycles and beards in pickup trucks?
Chico with pretenses of an academic presence?
Chico with life in the quiet lane?
Chico with elm trees and mulberry bushes?
Chico with a line on California?
A dotted line leading back past the hardware store, the pizza
joint, through the almond orchards and the giant kiwi
bush to the spot where Alberta played on the grass as an infant
before sailing back to Italy without her father?
Where Dad played pugilist with his Italian family?
Chico where he stood in front of the gym for a photograph
in his letterman jacket with Grandpa Foster?
Chico where invisible generations of farmworkers poured sweat
into the land to make the hills golden?
Chico where Indians broke the points of arrowheads & faded
from the highway?
Chico where 99 runs by Paradise?
Chico whose autumnal green light filters through quaint promises
of retirement tourists' brochures on loan from the bank?
Chico for seasons of students with bicycular dreams of summer?
Chico for part-time athletes and musicos with swelling thighs &
politics of relaxation, California-style?
Chico with food stamps for extra people with hair?
Chico with plywood houses, gas stations & fast food pointing

northeast to Deer Creek?
Chico with a corner of California torn off the road map?
Chico basically of sound mind in line with the founding fathers
of Fresno & Bakersfield?
Chico like a cute mole on the back of the great Central Valley?
Chico with all of that and the L.A. Times, too? Drugs & music, too?
Chico without a railroad of history going to any destination anywhere?
Chico with a Republican congressman and the smell of the wet
mountains in its hair?
Chico with a breeze, Chico of the West?

PACIFIC COAST VINDICATORY

For Alberta Buell Foster (Northway)
(1904–1985)

1.

Your eyelids slight membranes
before the daylight
almost hold a warm light
of their own against the dry
chilling of the evening.
Was the day itself so hot?
Leaning on the wall outside,
the plumb morning sunshine
through your bedroom window.
Like a young man in the afternoon
it touched the African violets
in the livingroom. They've
been doing fine now,
for some time better than you,
your visitors comment
on the bright blooms, while
your flesh slips through your
fingers. It's you who've
survived two husbands; cancer
took Floyd Northway, too.
The big green oxygen tanks cannot
substitute now for the years
you spent locked alone inside
his house in Vallejo. Alberta,
your eyes are as clear
as the still Santa Barbara noon,
reflected as it is in the State
Street storefront plateglass.
But the daylight does not nourish
this waiting of yours, and it's
your body being taken away from you,
draining into the colostomy bag.

2.
Alberta, the thin, pale Neopolitan woman
smokes a cigarette. She lives
in Naples now, nobody quite knows
where. You haven't seen her since
she was an infant, taken back
to Italy—but as your first
granddaughter she bears your name.
This news will be some time
in reaching her. By then
you'll be in the fields
of Santa Rosa
with the Mare Island
police/grandfather wearing khaki
in those old photos in your livingroom,
on the table amidst the violets.
Easy for your eyes to find you keep
photographs of the two boys
on the bureau: when they were young
together, in their uniforms
after the war.
They've come
a good stretch of road to see you,
sitting by your bed. (Ray's hair
whiter than your own. Jim
weighing the bitter arrangements.)
Ray's children, we bring our
children to see you.
They're no longer allowed to play
your organ, not to disturb
the quiet into which the street
hardly enters anymore. Your great
grandchildren go out beyond you,
to wheel below the Santa Ynez range
along the coastline like gulls.
Grandchildren the age of your sons

in the black and white photographs
next to the mirror, who kneel
in the geraniums growing for that
generation. Or at least,
for the day.

3.
The day after your memorial in Santa Barbara
we marched with ten thousand down Broadway
protesting U.S. imperialism in Central America.
It had been cold all day, with the wind
blowing down the dirty streets.
I didn't like to think of you
sitting in the easy chair all those
years. "How's Grandma," they'd ask—
never having gone themselves—I'd
shrug, "Waiting to die."
Cops patrolled on horseback, and in pairs
hassled the crowd of derelicts and
shoppers, checking for I.D.s,
while beyond the marchers a Guatemalan
Indian woman in filthy colorful costume
pulled along two kids, a girl crying,
an infant strapped to her back.
You had smiled, "I've really done it
this time." Thousands marched up
under the trees to the steps of City Hall,
where a drunk slept on his face
through the speeches. Some of us
walked down into Little Tokyo, past
Union Church, fenced off, abandoned,
for cheap Japanese food and hot tea.
The wind carried the dusty chill.
It must have been a goddamned boring
cold day there in Santa Rosa.

4.
South of Gaviota Pass on 101
heading toward Santa Barbara
those stands of eucalyptus on the hills
descending into the ocean. Originally
wood lots and windbreaks, incapable
as lonely foreigners of self-
propagation, relying on the hands
of men to sow those groves.
In their tall endurance they remind
me of you, fragrant before storms
on the sloping land, leafy green
shadows on the smooth pale trunks
above the curving blue Pacific.

VISITATION

1.

the desert sky obvious: clean
and clear above the owens valley.
the disparate cottonwoods reach
down through percolating soil, lean
into space in their wait
for the melt or infrequent rain,
leaves fluttering greenly
in today's breeze. in august
or september cotton may drift
over the gravel.
at manzanar
there's a graveyard for those
permanently relocated
'for their own protection' and a stone
marker erected after the fact.
you deviate from 395,
you leave footprints before
the winter winds. beyond
the car there's no electric cord
to hold, plug you into their rage
forgotten or forbidden, out of all
practicality placed behind them now.
just this mark enroute
lives took (unsung they remain
behind the billboards of popular
songs of daily broadcast) taking the silence
home
as cottonwoods take lightning
to ground,
crack, splinter
and burn. all winter
leafless, they're frozen under
the black clouds.

the people have gone,
they have turned back to
their work.

2.
those sleeping in the land
in the creosote bush and ashen dust
swirling around the big stones
are beckoning to you and you
are beckoning to them
with your memory

your remember the names
you read of the camp and the travelers,
what happened here when the ribcage
of the home was finally pulled free
from the backbone of the spirit,
and the dates when the heart here
ended.

3.
they were needed for cheap labor,
but no way were they the only
ones, or even the first.
agribusiness required a constant surplus
with wages controlled: the mexicans
and chicanos deported, families split
by train when the war ended.
oakies and arkies had been absorbed
by the growth of the military-industrial plant.
chained to trees and blowtorched
in poverty the oppression of rural blacks
an exodus to the inner city,
labor reserves. the chinese had been hounded
off the land into picturesque ghettos
for piecework in local sweatshops.

indians, hindus, mexicans, and white people, too,
in the fields, and filipino men (men
alone) stooped beside them.
the short-handled hoe. native americans corraled
far out on the land in houses like dog houses
while stray dogs starved. who spent
those years imprisoned for who they were?
who drove the bullet-nosed chevy
parked outside the TV home?
who had the cushy job, wife at home
getting anxious about the uppity
teenagers?
did the g.i. bill of a generation
whose parents would've voted for roosevelt
stop them from asking whose interests the state
reflects?
who benefited?
in the rows of strawberries, spinach and spruce vegetables
it was human beings,
this time japanese,
who were made
redundant.

4.
PASSPORT FOR THOSE WHOSE IDENTITY
HAS BEEN OFFICIALLY REMOVED

immigrant
through barbwire
child of the cold dawn,
your destiny runs in all directions
ice crystals forming in the ruts
where the puddles freeze over
(a sea of mud in the spring,
a plain of dust each summer)
the season turns on you and your
children,

the belongings proletarian, foresaken
by history, but not by
racists for their gain.
this was why they made the law.
asian exclusion act.
anti-mescegenation laws.
japanese could not own land.
these are not my words:
mere facts rising above ancestry.
what was done:
turn your back on the past,
it is theirs, their private property,
codified / coagulant in the lines
and scars on the maps of the skin.
face forward / face the future.
they will get the line of your jaw
along your shoulder.
that's good enough
for them.

5.
soldiers conducted the music of transport,
slow march to the dirge
sung on desert winds,
poston, arizona.
they'd say bureaucratic victims of "war
hysteria." lies: racism.
the only giddiness in the hatred
was in the shuffle and denial
of the cover-up.
(the soviets with their 20 million dead and humphrey's
bill to build new concentration camps for communists
for the cold war of u.s. hegemony
on top of the world, entering the space age)
while the shakuhachi note of issei sorrow
practically lost through the war,

though the war on fascism was won—
with blood in other
bloody homelands, but not won at home.

soldier's death in the distance brought
medals, paper, flowers, to rest on
little black and white photographs
of our faces and our people standing
against the wall, but the flowers
from la jornada del muerte blew atomic
petals across the dawns

6.
OKAY?
*Based on a photograph by Dorothea Lange of a Nisei girl sitting on baggage
before the departure*

under that calm wing of black
hair your dark eyes watch
in wait, glance sharply above
the collar of the thick
winter coat you wear,
wool in may, since you must
carry everything yourself
now, and tag it with your
number

it was only a matter of years, mother,
before you freshened your face
in ordinary storefront windows.
it was only years, grandfather,
before you walked this sidewalk
stooped as if from strawberries
like any other american.
child, tagged like baggage,
your black eyes watched that
highway of silence

7.
jeff told billy and me,
"i never killed anybody,
i didn't put the indians on reservations,
i didn't take away their land.
i don't hate black people.
where i live there ain't any
black people. i didn't put no japanese
people in concentration camps.
i was only twelve when the vietnam
war ended. i didn't kill any babies.
it ain't my fault. besides,
all that shit is
over with."

billy said, "the thing that shocked me
most was when i heard that black people
could not be on the same baseball team.
that's what i remember most."

after the summer in colorado
spent fighting forest fires, jeff went back
to college in bemidji, billy went back
to the university in fort collins,
and i went to look for work
in seattle.

8.
the towers disappear from the brush,
the iron barbs oxidize in time
and drift into the sand.
the mountains still rise pink
in the sunrise above the site.
you can stand there yourself
to see,
you can stand anywhere you want
and still see.

NOTES:

nisei: second generation
issei: first generation
shakuhachi: Japanese bamboo flute
la jornada del muerte: site, called Trinity, of the first atom bomb blast,
July 16, 1946

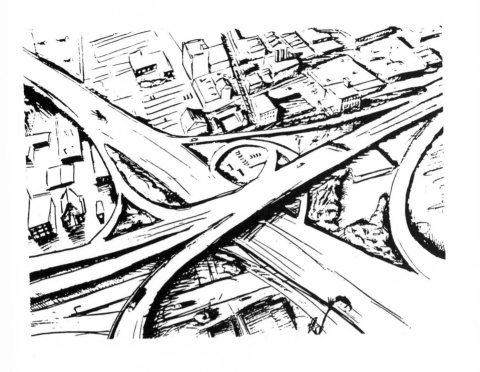

AFTERWORD

A NOTE ON FORM

In the upper left-hand corner of the square of Colorado is Brown's Park. The Rockies lift Colorado like the immense spinal column of our continent, but west of Brown's Park the country descends into desert, the vast, beautiful rainshadow, the Great Basin winter-cold desert of Utah and Nevada. All the blue mountains in the distance constantly visible, there in the edge of your vision, are covered by evergreen pine, spruce, fir, and aspen, but the rugged broken country around Brown's Park is pinon/juniper land.

It looks parklike in summer. Come up on it along the two-lane strip of asphalt, past muddy streams washing silt into the Green River, where I've seen golden eagles scavenging roadkills on the dotted line . . . the rolling stretches of sagebrush dappled with cloud shadows under rugged ridges and eroded washes. Under that big sky, the sagebrush is clean and pungent when you walk out into it. Fragrant, and a tough pastel green, yellow-green, or light gray, tipped with fine silver in the brilliant high desert summer sunlight.

So beautiful—you could almost forget the rest, rape and murder every other minute, the torture and abuse of children, the nuclear weapons hidden in scattered pockets all across this land. In the last century Brown's Park achieved some infamy as a remote Robber's Roost hideout for cattle thieves and bandits preying on the ranch land to the southeast. Nowadays the park looks peaceful enough amid its surrounding buttes, mesas and plateaus, but any real winter weather can put an end to serious illusions regarding its character. A close look at the form and texture of a pinon trunk can give you an idea of the endurance necessary to survive here.

The Green River curls through the park and cuts a gorge in impressive oxbows through Dinosaur National Monument, before heading back into the hot country in Utah. On a dirt track that runs past a single-room store with outhouses in back and a gas pump in front, forking off to a copper mine in the hills, there's a Bureau of Land Management fire patrol camp. At least once a month we'd be on patrol, driving the ridge road to the little trailer under a Douglas fir, out on the road which went up to Zenobia Peak, fire lookout over the monument and Utah to the west. My crew was usually college kids out for the summer, and we drove a big six-wheel-drive vehicle which carried two pumps and 300 gallons on the back, along with a box of chainsaw, shovels, axes, other tools, and our packs.

Every summer lightning storms blow over the land, touching off a few fires here and there, as has happened for eons. But it was only during this century that bureaucrats evolved who decided that all these fires needed to be stomped out, in order to protect the rights of logging companies and oil transnationals to exploit public land at their convenience. You might say we risked life and limb to secure their privilege in this occasionally hard, dangerous work, but it was one of the only jobs I've really enjoyed. Fighting fires.

After a couple of seasons in the area, without any formal training, they gave me a little red card that said "Squad Boss: Training Needed" and put me in charge of the truck and a crew. I taught a couple college kids to fight fires and we went right to work on some Forest Service land up in the Rockies, where we worked twenty-hour shifts through the billowing smoke, into the light of the moon. After four days a summer storm came up and put the fire out, and as we left the big truck crushed a culvert and sank axle-deep in a stream, but soon we got sent back into the dry country on patrol again. It was a good way to see the country, places nobody else ever saw, outside a few ranchers and hunters.

With little to do besides radio checks and weather reports, I showed my crew the high country. When there were no storms in the area, I'd drive up into the mountains following the dotted lines on topo maps. Never mind it might dead-end us somewhere with the big truck nose-first down a staircase of boulders, the water sloshing out forward from the tanks, with no route out of the cul-de-sac and the jeep trail on the map long since washed out or overgrown, and us so low on fuel that we never could have made a fire call without a side trip somewhere for gas. We were lucky.

We rotated patrols with other pumper truck crews, out in the Piceance Basin, the oil town of Rangely, Craig at headquarters, and Brown's Park. I learned to shoot dice from a Mexican crew brought up from Durango to clean up the last of a big fire, and we cleaned them out of fifty dollars. At the end of the season when the helicopter crew had gone back to the university, helicopters ferried us to mountaintops inaccessible to vehicles, where we put fires out on a slant, with only the water we could carry and our chainsaws and shovels—cutting out a landing area so the helicopter could lift us off again. One ridge was so narrow that the helicopter teetered back and forth in the breeze, the blades nearly touching the trees as we pulled up and then dropped down into a beautiful whitewater gorge.

And certainly, by the last year I was there, these college kids played out sophisticated sexual soap operas at headquarters and in the field, which usually involved the dispatcher, so you could keep up on it in code in radio traffic. Most of the crew was white kids from soft suburban homes and more money than I was used to, and I never did get to be part of the more exclusive cliques in town. Most of 'em thought I was kind of weird, always reading about shit that didn't have a goddamned thing to do with getting through college and getting a better job in the future. But in the field I always had a crew that took care of its fire line, who could direct putting out a fire without anybody getting hurt, and who could get there without getting lost. (We had lots of map experience. We already knew some of the roads.) We ate ashes for a week on end, getting three or four hours sleep a night on the big ones, grimy and sooty from head to foot, chopping fire lanes through the trees, high on adrenalin and fatigue, watching huge flames pour sparks into the stars, and then, as the job wound up, the quiet of the forest regain the slopes.

And poetry?

The work demanded you knew who could give you good directions over the radio, and straight information on the ground when you were heading into a big new fire, and you had to know who could be counted on not to send you alone into something you couldn't handle, and who could take care of themselves and their co-workers. You had to know who could take care of their crews and not hit them with a chainsaw out of fatigue and carelessness. All summer long we'd be talking to people we'd gotten to know well, like it or not—together for 24 hours a day, sleeping in the same dirty clothes on the ground, getting our food from the same boxes, sharing water, shooting the shit. I went through some of my stories, narratives and theories more than once. There was a lot of funny bullshit and honesty over late-night poker games before the deal went down.

And poetry?

There was a mountain above Brown's Park to the north, where the antelope fled across the slopes at the approach of the vehicle and the breeze spun the aspen leaves. You could see across the trees to where the land broke up in Wyoming with the clouds moving south, trailing a dark wash of rain and the sunlight breaking occasionally on the mountainside. And up around the mountain you could see west from the uppermost left-hand corner of Colorado, the Green River flowing below into the Colorado Plateau, and then, riding across the top of the mountain through green summer grass, you had to slow for a herd of elk galloping across the road, their hooves thumping the ruts into mud as they went past the water hole, big as horses. The sky bringing on another lightning storm or breaking up for clearer weather—and me, I'd be talking loud over the grind of the engine and the six-wheel drive and the radio static. I'd be getting the crew laughing and shouting, or maybe just quiet, staring with partial disbelief, though they knew I'd give it to 'em straight as I saw it, wondering.

For me, this was poetry enough, given the country.

This is what workers are doing everywhere. Given the circumstances (like an absence of lead-assed management and stupid anxious hostility) you're gonna find somebody bullshitting, acting human, acting out feeling alive in the best of senses. I worked in banks watering plants and listened to clerks yak on the phone, tired of counting other people's money, telling the stories of their romances in subtle, ironic dialogue: "And then he called me up Friday, what he said then is . . . . So I go . . . . And then he tells me . . . ." I worked as a printer in Seattle and listened to the groundskeepers kick back behind the buildings telling stories and bad jokes, about the neighbor who bought an Impala for the tires for 100 and drove it for a year to Canada and back before reselling it for 500 on the same tires. In spite of all the dumb shit and bad ideas out there, people everywhere, from the Shoshone-Arapaho and Mexican crews on big fires in Wyoming and Colorado, to those I sold oysters to in San Francisco's Chinatown, to the strippers in Palo Alto who gave me a crowbar to keep behind the door on my job as a bouncer, I always figured the workers had great stories to tell about their hard times, their hassles and their friends, their leisure, their ideas and what they thought they were doing with their lives. It's going down now.

I took what I could learn from this for the form in my poems, plus what I've read. I emphasize a narrative tendency, because it's something I'm used to, like I say. It's something I hear workers doing, something I pay attention to. It's how we get the word. It's how we find out what's really going on at a job site. Sometimes it's just gossip, with some backdoor experts getting the goods on everybody in the whole neighborhood, but other times it might be real threats with dangerous consequences, and we all pay attention. We all work here. . . .

I like the ready recognition that comes through narrative direction, without sacrificing the directness and exactitude of poems. In terms of a poetic tradition, what workers say in lunchrooms or over coffee first thing in the morning may not be formally recognized as such, but I grew up with it, with what people say over a cold beer on the porch. I operate with it, I relate to it, like most of us do, working our way through. I hope my work is some tribute to the people who struggle on.

And, sure, besides accompanying workers who do not consider themselves poets, or even any kinds of students of human experience, who do not really practice poetry in any oral tradition, though their lives require the utmost creativity to keep the clarity and warmth of their spirit and intellect alive, I read poems all the time. And in poetry I see an immense diversity of content, purpose and form, and much to be admired everywhere. Lots of poets bring forth from their experience and imparted traditions formal qualities which make their work fascinating and instructive. Many poets speak not only from their experiences as Blacks or Chicanos, for example, but also use this cultural focus to inform their consciousness of working class life. It's a damned big country in that way, too! Such formal diversity speaks of the intense, striving work moving ahead across a rough country. We got people all around us laboring to make this culture live and stand up for a fight. It gestures to the future, like flagging on a road. Smoke rising on the horizon, messages starting to come in . . .

Sesshu Foster

There's a directness in these poems, an immediacy, a sense of having been personally addressed and involved; there's eloquence even in the everyday; and there's irony among the anger. This man has been reached by injustice, and he did not fail to reach me with it.

—John Sanford